"A sweet story that helps kids find their true 'north' as they pursue the path of faith."

CLAUDIA CANGILLA MCADAM, Catholic Media Awards winner
and author of *Mother Cabrini: A Heart for the World*, commissioned
by Angel Studios and published by Sophia Institute Press

"Tammy Fernando's second book, *Lost Until the Light Comes*, reminds us of our need for each other and for the guidance of our Good Shepherd.

"A sweet story with lovely illustrations clearly created by someone with children!"

SYLVIA DORHAM, author of *The Monks' Daily Bread*

"Chris is persuaded to go on a journey to Beyond-Blue-Land. He has his compass, but it is no protection against the danger he encounters. In his great need he asks God to help him; he sees the Light and is safe.

"Getting lost is a situation with which many children can identify. *Lost Until the Light Comes* is a simple story of a young boy's discovery of the closeness of Father, Son and Holy Spirit at a moment of great vulnerability: he is lost and is found."

ANN HIGGS, former primary school headteacher

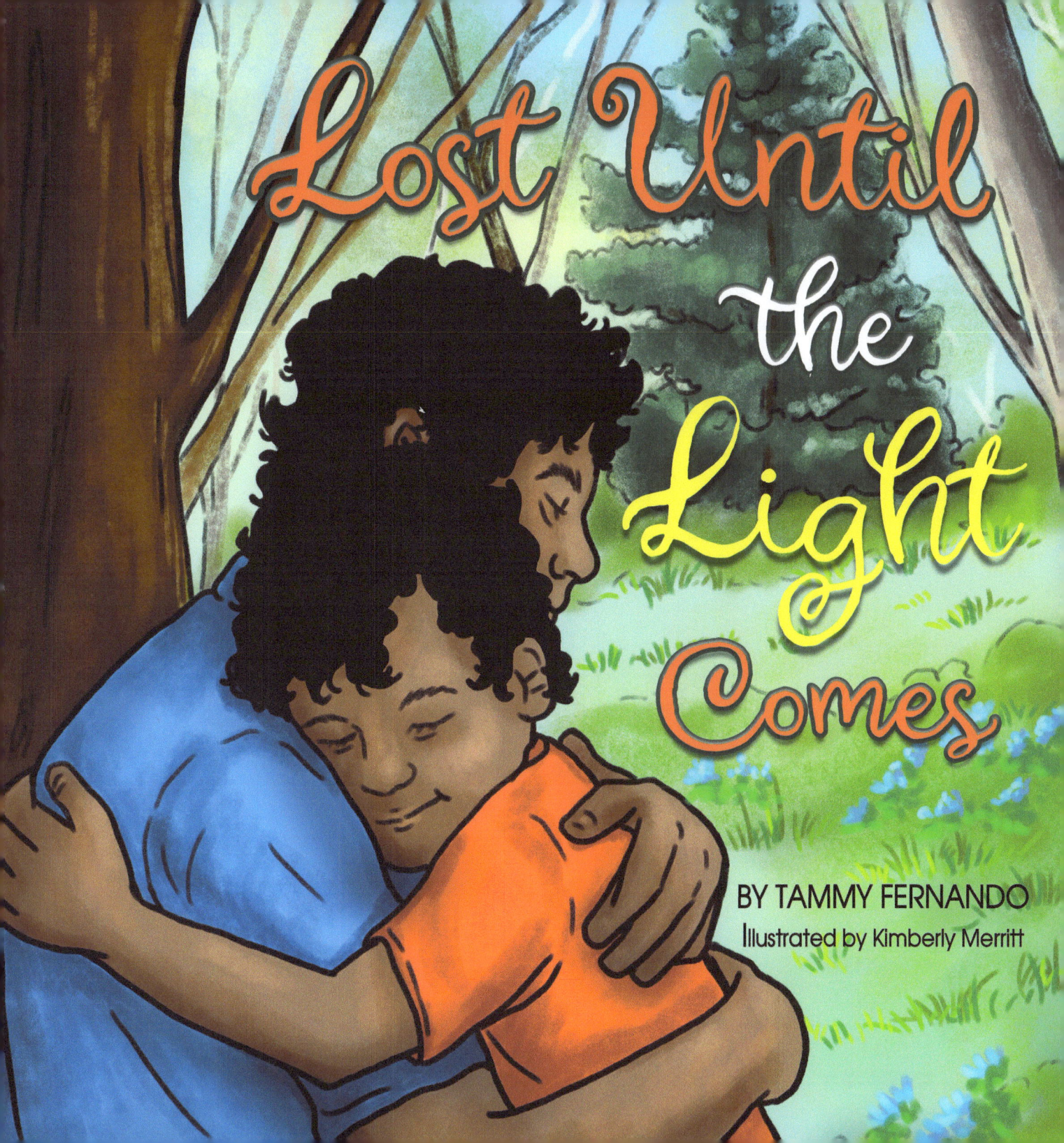

Lost Until the Light Comes by Tammy Fernando. All rights reserved © 2024. No portion of this book may be reproduced, stored in a retrieval system, or transmitted in any form or by any means, except for brief quotations in printed reviews, without prior permission from the author.

ISBN: 978-1-7392724-1-8

Editing, formatting, and cover by ChristianEditingandDesign.com.
Illustrations by Kimberly Merritt.

Scripture taken from the New King James Version®. Copyright © 1982 by Thomas Nelson. Used by permission. All rights reserved.

Heaven is our Home
www.tammyfernando.co.uk

Dedicated to the Most Holy Trinity

Thanks to Kim Merritt, Shannon Herring, Dixie Phillips and Bethany Clark for all their creative talents in birthing this second book for me!

The front door slowly swings open on its own.

"Shani!" Chris exclaims.

"Hi, Chris!" Shani giggles and continues, "Hi, Mr. Fernandez! My mum is in your kitchen. She has got a surprise for you all!"

Chris' gaze moves from Shani to his dad. *What surprise can this be?*

As he walks into the kitchen, the sweet, spicy smell of chai tea fills the air and covers him like a big hug. Here he finds his mummy, Shani's mum and Zanna.

"Darling," Chris' mum smiles at her husband. "Myriam has won a pilgrimage to Beyond-Blue-Land and she can take another family as part of the prize! What do you think? Shall we go?"

Chris' daddy thinks for a moment. "Well, it sounds alright to me. What do you think, Chris?"

Chris shrugs and stares at the floor.

"I don't want to go!" Chris blurts out. "What about Devon and using my compass to find our way through the woods?"

Shani's mum explains, "You could still use your compass to cross the large wood and find the famous Blue Mountain...."

"Look! It's blue!" exclaims Zanna. "I wish I could walk in this picture...." She stares into space and sighs dreamily.

"Okay then. I'll go!"

God the Father grins, God the Son, Jesus, prays, and God the Holy Spirit whispers, "I love you" into Chris' heart.

The plane touches down on the Beyond-Blue-Land tarmac with a bump.

"Yes, Chris, that's right. Now just adjust your compass so that the red needle is pointing north ... that's right ... and northeast is this way." Dad points.

A big smile spreads across his face as Chris finds north.

"Let's play hide-and-seek!" Zanna shouts.

"Yes! Let's!" Ozz cheers.

Orr covers his eyes and counts. "Okay! I'm counting to thirty. One . . . two . . . three . . ."

"Be careful and don't go too far!" warns Chris' dad.

"Make sure that you can always see us!" Shani's dad adds his warning.

"We will!" says Shani.

"Twenty-nine, thirty!" Orr starts looking for clues. "Found you! Both your shoes were sticking out!"

"You were pushing me!" Zanna yells over her shoulder.

"That's because you were pushing me!" Ozz hollers back.

"Aitchoo! Aitchoo!"

Orr bends down to Shani's face. "I can hear you!" says Orr.

But where is Chris?

"Chris! Chris!" they call.

Where is my Chris?

Chris' mum widens her eyes and furrows her brow.

"Let's pray!" Orr exclaims. Mum's lips form a gentle smile as she presses her hands together in prayer.

Jesus! Please bring my son back to me!

At that moment, Ozz finds Chris' empty shoes stuck in the mud. When Chris' mummy sees her son's shoes, she feels her eyes fill with tears. She cups her mouth with her hands and cries out, "Chris! Chris! Where are you?"

Chris suddenly realises that he should stop chasing the squirrels and get back to the game. He looks all around but can't see anyone.

"Mum! Dad!" he calls into the woodland air. Silence. *How can I get back to everyone? My shoes! They will lead me back....*

Very scared, Chris tries to retrace his footsteps.

After trudging down the path for a long time, Chris still doesn't see anyone else. He hears the wind blow through the leaves. He hasn't heard human voices for so long. What can he do now?

SNAP!

Chris gasps!

SNAP!

This time the snap is farther away.

SNAP!

Chris hears a fierce growling sound in the distance....

God the Father protects. God the Son, Jesus, prays as a warrior. God the Holy Spirit lets Chris feel His closeness.

Chris feels tears streaming down his cheeks. "God, help me! Please help me!"

He lifts up his head and sees a faint light just outside the tree hollow. He pokes his head outside and watches the light grow.

"CHRIS, FOLLOW ME!" says the comforting Voice.

What is that golden light? Don't I know that voice from somewhere? Chris hurries down the tree trunk....

"CHRIS, FOLLOW ME!" The Voice speaks again.

Chris suddenly knows whose voice it is!

It is Jesus' voice!
Chris follows the light.

After a short while the light disappears, and Chris finds himself at the edge of the woods.

Suddenly, he hears his mum's voice. "Chris!" she yells loudly. "Oh Chris, I'm so glad that we have found you!" Everyone hugs and kisses Chris.

"Chris, we were so worried about you! You must never wander off like that again!" Dad speaks sternly.

"I'm sorry." Chris brushes a hot tear from his cheek. "I was following the squirrels and then I got lost! Then the wolf came! I started crying and asking God to help me. A light came and a voice said, 'Chris! Follow Me!' I think it was Jesus. I followed Him, and that's how I am here!"

Chris' dad gathers him up in his big arms. "Chris, I'm sure that was Jesus. It's amazing that He spoke to you in that way, but *please* don't wander off again."

"I won't, Dad." Chris buries his face in his daddy's chest.

God the Father is happy.

God the Son, Jesus, praises the Father.

God the Holy Spirit speaks into Chris' heart. Chris feels loved.

The Lord is my Shepherd.
Psalm 23

Tammy Fernando

Tammy Fernando is the author of *Lost Until the Light Comes:* her second book in a six-part series of Christian fiction books for young children. Tammy is honoured that the Lord has asked her to embark on a career in writing and excited to have the opportunity to guide children to the heart of God. Her books emphasise two things she feels the Lord wants her to convey to little ones: the need for a personal relationship with our Creator-God and the continual presence and help of the Holy Trinity.

Outside of writing, Tammy enjoys baking for friends, family and most recently for her first author event held at her parish in Beckenham, Kent. She also enjoys the creativity and buzz she finds whenever she gets the chance to sing or dance.

Kimberly Merritt

Illustrator Kimberly Merritt has been a pastor's wife for over twenty years. While serving beside her husband and homeschooling her four children, she has been blessed to have illustrated over sixty children's books for authors all over the world. Kim loves to paint, play guitar, and write about her walk with the Lord. You can read more about her at https://landofharvest.com/home/art/.